Carlin Lock 796.332

Gr. 4 Up

QUARTERBACK

ALSO BY GEORGE SULLIVAN

Run, Run Fast

George Sullivan

illustrated with photographs by the author

and line drawings by Don Madden

Thomas Y. Crowell New York

Library of Congress Cataloging in Publication Data
Sullivan, George, 1927–
  Quarterback.

  Summary: Discusses what it takes to become a quarterback, how to train with weights, how to pass and handle
the ball, and how to improve one's performance.
  1. Quarterback (Football)—Juvenile literature.
[1. Quarterback (Football) 2. Football] I. Madden, Don,
1927–   ill.   II. Title.
GV951.3.S95 1982   796.332′25   81–43889
ISBN 0–690–04241–8   AACR2
ISBN 0–690–04242–6 (lib. bdg.)

1 2 3 4 5 6 7 8 9 10
First Edition

Contents

Acknowledgements

Many people helped in the preparation of this book. The author is especially grateful to the Enfield Starrs of Enfield, Connecticut, for their enthusiastic cooperation. Special thanks are due Fred Semanie, athletic director; C. J. Daigle, director of operations; head coaches Phil Bellico and Chip Riley; and the many team members who posed for photographs. The author is also grateful to Francesca Kurti, T.L.C. Custom Labs, Bob Healy, Aime LaMontagne, and Bill Sullivan.

QUARTERBACK

Credit: Aime La Montagne

1 Before You Begin

When his team wins, the quarterback gets cheered. When things go wrong, he hears boos. The quarterback is the most important player on the field.

It's easy to understand why.

The quarterback is the player who takes command on the field. He sets formations and calls plays.

The quarterback handles the ball on every play. He either hands off to another back or throws a pass. Sometimes he runs with the ball himself.

Playing quarterback is one of the most difficult jobs in sports.

What It Takes

As the quarterback, you have to be quick. You have to have quick hands and quick feet. Since you control the ball on every play, your quickness determines the speed with which your team attacks.

As the quarterback, you also have to be smart. You must know the duties of each of your teammates on every play. You must know the strengths and weaknesses of the opposing team. Using this knowledge, you must choose the plays and strategy that will defeat the opposition.

Your attitude is important, too. In every game, you must have your heart set on winning and do everything in your power to accomplish it. Coaches call this "desire."

It's also up to the quarterback to get the other players on the team to develop this will to win. This takes leadership. Becoming a leader is no easy job. First, you have to be confident in yourself. Then you must set an example for other team members. You have to work harder than anyone else during team practice sessions. You have to know how to play your position down to the smallest detail. You have to take pride in being physically fit. There are no shortcuts to becoming a leader.

It can take many years to become a good quarterback, and the competition is tough because many boys want to play the position.

That's why you should learn the other skills that football requires. Learn how to catch passes. Learn how to block. In other words, become a complete player while you continue to work at becoming a quarterback. Develop all the skills the position demands. But, at the same time, be ready to play another position on the team. Remember, playing *some* position is better than not playing at all.

Getting a Physical Exam

Football is a rough game. It makes tough demands on the human body. You must be in top physical condition to play. Before you take up the sport, see your family or school doctor to get a complete medical examination.

Your Equipment

Football demands proper equipment. Your most important piece of equipment is your helmet. Always wear your helmet, even in light workouts with your friends. Your helmet should feel as natural to wear as your jersey or socks.

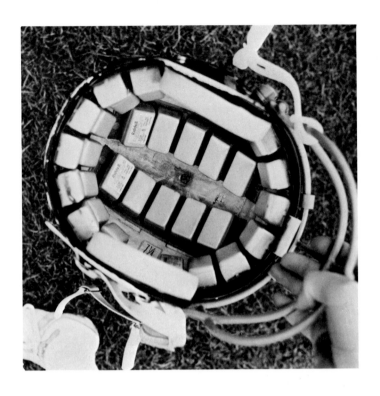

Inside the helmet, there should be a web of straps. Your head should fit snugly into the webbing. And there should be plenty of space between the webbing and the helmet's hard plastic top. Also, you must have space between your ears and the helmet sides. Be sure the helmet fits properly. If it's too tight, it won't protect you because it won't absorb the impact of the blows your head receives. If the helmet is loose, it's just as bad. It can be slammed down on the bridge of your nose, cutting it, or it can be knocked off when you're tackled, leaving your head unprotected.

Check your helmet's fit by placing your index finger between your forehead and the front of the helmet. There should be just enough space for the finger. If you can easily move your finger back and forth, the helmet is too big. If the finger has to be forced into the space, the helmet is too tight. In addition, the helmet's ear holes should line up exactly with the openings of your ears.

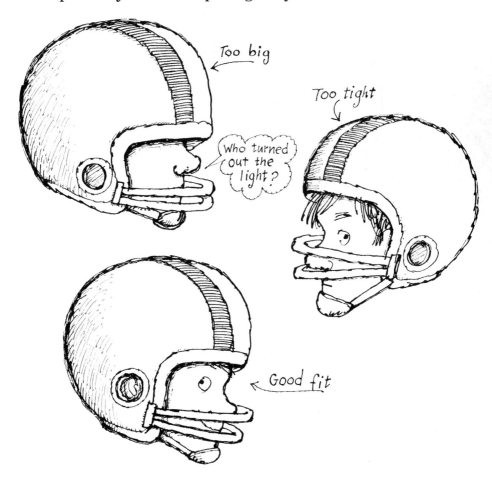

The helmet should be fitted with a face guard to protect your nose and mouth. Be sure the face guard doesn't block your vision. If it does, have it adjusted.

A teeth protector is vital, too. In fact, you will not be allowed in an official game without it. One end attaches to your face guard, and you bite down on the other end.

A chin strap holds the helmet firmly to the head. Never go onto the field with the chin strap unfastened. A blow to the head could easily knock the helmet off.

Never borrow anyone else's helmet. You're almost certain to get a bad fit. A helmet that doesn't fit right can be about as dangerous as no helmet at all.

Besides a helmet, you should also wear:

Shoulder Pads—These are made of a hard surface of molded plastic backed by a cushioned layer of foam rubber. They should be big enough to cover your shoulders but still permit you to swing your arms freely. They should cover your collarbone, too.

Rib Pads; Hip Pads—These protect you from blows from the side when you're getting set to pass. They're made of padded foam rubber.

Thigh and Knee Pads—Also made of foam rubber, these fit into specially designed pockets in your pants.

A long tuck-in jersey, knee socks, and cleated shoes complete the uniform.

Warming Up

Be sure to take the time to loosen up your muscles before every practice session or game. On very cold days, take a longer time than usual. Warm up gradually.

Begin your warm-up session with some light jogging. Then do some simple stretching exercises. For instance, stand erect with your hands on your hips. Lean forward from the waist. Lean to the left. Lean back. Lean to the right.

Toe touches are also good for warming up. Stand erect with your feet wide apart. Put your hands out to your sides. Without bending your knees, lean over and touch your right hand to your left toe. Go back to your original position. Then bend over and touch your left hand to your right toe.

Loosen your leg muscles with what's called the "hurdler's stretch." Sit down with legs outstretched. Bend your left leg to your side, doubling it over like a jackknife. Keep the right leg straight. Bend forward from the waist, reaching to grasp your right foot with your hands. Then reverse the position of your legs. Reach with your hands to grasp your left foot.

Never fail to warm up. "Cold" muscles are easily injured. Such injuries are painful and they take many weeks to heal..

2 Handling the Ball

In handling the ball, the quarterback has to be quick; he has to be sure.

Calling the Signals

Every play begins when the quarterback calls the snap signal. The signal is a number. Usually it is number one, two, or three.

For example, in the huddle, the quarterback may say, "On three!" That means the quarterback is to snap the ball when he calls out three.

After the teams have lined up, the quarterback shouts out the snap signal. If the ball is to be snapped on three, he'll shout, "One! Two! Three!"

Many teams use the word "hut" as part of the snap signal. If the ball is to be snapped on three, the quarterback will yell, "Hut one! Hut two! Hut three!"

Be sure to announce the signals in a clear, crisp voice. You must sound confident. You must sound like a leader.

In the huddle keep your head up. Look at your teammates; don't look down at the ground. Give instructions clearly. Don't mumble. If you have special instructions for a player, look directly at him. You might say to a lineman, for example, "Really get in there and block." Look him right in the eye as you talk to him. It's a good bet he'll get the job done.

Taking the Snap

Get up close to the center. Spread your feet about shoulder width apart. Bend at the waist. Bend at the knees slightly. But don't stoop over. Keep your chin up. You have to be able to look over the defense. You must be comfortable as you await the snap. You must be ready to turn to either your right or left as you move back.

Position your hands to receive the ball. Place the heel of the right hand against the heel of the left. Then bring your thumbs together so they touch from end to end. Your hands are like an open clamshell.

As you take your stance, the right hand should be the top hand. Place the back of the right hand against the center's crotch. The left hand is below the right. The center uses your right hand as his target in delivering the ball.

Thwack! The center delivers the ball into your right hand. Clamp your left hand onto the ball from below.

Practice receiving the snap over and over. It should always be fast. It should always be smooth. You and the center should work together like a well-oiled machine.

Handing Off

After he takes the snap, the quarterback's job is usually to hand off to a running back. Every handoff should be quick and sure.

Suppose you've just received the ball from the center. As the center charges ahead to block for you, turn away from him so you can see the runner coming. Bring the ball to your belly. Now you've got the ball in both hands. The runner is driving toward you.

Focus your eyes on the runner's belly. That's where you're going to put the ball. Hold the ball in one hand and place it in the pocket the runner has formed with his arms. Don't slam the ball there. You might cause the runner to juggle it. Just lay the ball into his arms gently.

Practice handoffs with a center and running back. Have the runner line up to your left. Take the snap from center. Turn and place the ball in the runner's arms. Then have the runner line up on the right side. Repeat the drill.

You can also practice by yourself. Place a handkerchief or other marker behind you on the ground. This indicates the spot where the handoff is to take place. Then pretend you are taking the ball from the center, and move toward the marker as rapidly as you can. Keep practicing until your footwork is quick and smooth.

The Fake Handoff

Sometimes you'll want to try to trick the defense by faking a handoff. You keep the ball yourself, then pass it.

You have to be an actor to make the fake successful. Look at the runner who is driving toward you, his hands positioned to receive the ball. But your hand is empty. You're holding the ball in your other hand, hiding it at your hip. As you go back to pass, slide the ball toward your belly. Keep the ball hidden for as long as you can.

Another way to fake is to place the ball at the runner's belly, and then take it away. You're hoping the defensive players see the ball go in, but don't see it come out.

Pitching Out

The pitchout is a soft underhand toss to one of your runners. It cannot travel forward. That would be an illegal pass. It must travel backward or parallel to the line of scrimmage.

Let's suppose you've just taken the center's snap. Turn and take a step in the direction of the runner. Look at him. Using both hands let the ball fly. Remember, it's a gentle underhand throw. The runner will be moving fast. Aim in front of him. You don't want to make him slow down. That would ruin the play.

3 How to Pass

The forward pass is football's most exciting weapon. When the quarterback completes a pass, the play usually gains a big chunk of yardage.

Passing also helps the running game. When the defensive players are sitting back and waiting for the run, it's difficult for your team to get much yardage on the ground. But the opposition team can't sit back and wait once you, the quarterback, start completing passes. The team on defense has to start charging. And when that happens, a running play is a good play to call.

The Grip

You grip the ball with your fingers, not with
your whole hand. There should always be some
space between your palm and the surface of the
ball. Grip the ball toward the end with your
fingers spread. Try to place three fingers across
the laces. If you have a small hand, grip even
more toward the end of the ball. Place only two
fingers across the laces. Grip firmly. But don't
squeeze the ball.

Test your grip like this: Hold the ball beside your right ear as if you were going to throw it. Swing your arm back and forth several times. But don't release the ball. The ball should not work loose. If it does, adjust the grip so you have better control of the ball.

The Throw

Always take the time to warm up your arm. Start with short tosses. Don't throw hard passes until your arm feels loose.

Get set to throw by shifting your weight to your right foot. At the same time, raise the ball behind your head. Your elbow should be at the same level as your shoulder. Deliver the ball with an overhand throw. Your arm travels straight down. It's somewhat the same motion used to serve in tennis. You also use it in chopping a stick of wood with a hatchet.

As you deliver the ball, take a short stride forward with your left foot. Whip your arm forward and down, pushing off from your right foot. Release the ball high, somewhere above the level of your shoulders. A high release enables you to throw the ball far. It also has value dur-

ing a game. Enemy linemen are rushing toward you, trying to block the ball. Their arms are raised above their heads. By keeping the ball high, you're able to get it above their up-stretched hands.

Give your hand a quick twist to the right as you release the ball. Follow through with your arm and upper body. Your hand ends up at about the level of your knees. You're bent at the waist slightly. Your weight is concentrated on your left foot. This follow-through helps you to throw hard and makes your passes accurate.

Dropping Back to Pass

In a game, you must go back fast when you plan to pass. It's dangerous to stay up close to the line. You're sure to get grabbed and tackled. Once you get back, blockers will take up positions to protect you. The protected area is called the "pocket."

There are two ways to drop back. You can run with backward steps. Or you can turn and sprint back. When you run backward, you can see the entire field as you go. It's easy to spot a receiver. When you turn and sprint back, you can see only part of the field.

But there's a big disadvantage to running backward. The enemy players can see the ball clearly. They *know* you're going to pass. The better way is to turn and sprint back. When you go, look back over your shoulder. That way, you'll be able to see what your opponents are doing. They'll be looking at your back. They won't know that you're going to be passing until you turn forward and put your arm up. Turning and running also saves time. You travel much faster when you turn and sprint than when you backpedal.

No matter which method you rely upon, use your left hand as well as your right to control the ball. Keep both hands on the ball for as long as you can.

Different Types of Passes

Don't plan on throwing the ball the same way every time. Suppose you're passing to a runner who is darting out of the backfield. He's only a few yards from you. A soft pass is what's needed. Throw hard and he's sure to muff the catch.

To toss a soft pass, tilt the nose of the ball upward as you release it. Bring your arm forward slowly. It's something like throwing a dart.

Let's say you're going to pass to a receiver just beyond the line of scrimmage. There are sure to be many defenders in the area. The ball has to get to the receiver in a hurry. You have to throw as hard as you can.

Tilt the nose of the ball slightly downward as you release it. Move your arm fast. The ball will

bore its way to your receiver. Quarterbacks call this a "heavy" ball. It packs quite a wallop. Don't try such a pass unless you're throwing to a sure-handed receiver.

To throw a long pass, tilt the nose of the ball upward. Be sure to take a full stride as you release, and be sure to follow through.

When throwing a long pass, you have to get the ball well out in front of the receiver. You want him to be able to make the catch without breaking stride.

Never underthrow a long pass. The opposition is almost certain to intercept it. It's better to overthrow your target. The worst that can happen is that the ball won't be caught. An incompletion is always better than an interception.

Faking Passes

Knowing how to fake a pass is almost as important as knowing how to throw one.

Use your eyes and your arm to fake. Suppose you're planning to throw to a receiver on your right. First look to the left. Defensive backs are often trained to watch a quarterback's eyes. By looking to the left, you may cause them to move in that direction.

Also use your arm. Whip your arm forward as if to pass. But don't release the ball.

Watch the defensive players carefully. A lineman may hesitate for a split second. A defensive back may take a step in the wrong direction. One of your receivers gets free as a result. That's when you really throw.

Successful faking takes real acting ability. Push off from your right foot. Stride forward with the left foot. Pick out your "target." Wear a determined look. Do everything but send the ball on its way.

Make faking a part of your passing strategy. But don't fake exactly the same way every time. Sometimes fake once. Other times, fake twice. Still other times, don't fake at all; just throw. You've got to keep the defense guessing.

Mistakes Passers Make

A good pass travels in a tight spiral. But some passers throw a ball that wobbles in the air. A wobbly pass is seldom accurate. To get a pass that spirals, be sure to bring your arm and wrist straight down as you deliver the ball.

Other passers seem unable to throw the ball far. This is because their weight is on their front foot (their left foot) as they throw. You must push off your rear foot (the right foot) as you whip your arm through. Some coaches call the right foot the "power foot."

Still other passers throw the ball too far. It always goes beyond the target. This results from standing too straight. You must bend your knees slightly as you throw.

Some passing mistakes:

a wobbly pass

a pass that falls short

a pass that overshoots target

HEY! I'm the target!

Practicing

Some receivers are very fast. Some aren't. When you're throwing to a fast receiver, you have to be aware of his speed. You have to lead him more with the ball. Practice with your various receivers. That's the only way you can get to know what each is capable of doing.

To most quarterbacks, practicing passing is fun. But don't spend all of your time throwing the ball. Also practice taking the snap, handing off, pitching out, and all the other skills a quarterback must have.

4 How to Get Better

Practice passing with one knee on the ground. If you're right-handed, put the right knee to the ground. The left leg should be bent, the left foot flat to the ground. Throw the ball in the way described earlier in this book. Throw overhand, bringing the ball arm straight down from behind your head. This drill forces you to use your upper body and arm when throwing. It strengthens your arm and improves your grip.

Practicing Passing

Throwing a weighted ball will also help to strengthen your throwing arm and hand. Wrap the ball with black electrician's tape. Then try passing it. You don't have to throw the ball far. Short tosses will do the job.

Also try passing a basketball. To grip the basketball, you'll have to stretch your fingers wide apart. When you go back to throwing a football, it may be as easy to grip as a grapefruit.

When you go to school, carry a football with you. Practice gripping and releasing it, gripping and releasing it. Drop the ball and grab it with your throwing hand before it hits the ground.

To improve your accuracy, suspend an old tire from a tree limb or goalpost crossbar by means of a rope. Practice throwing the ball through the hole. Before each throw, get into your set position. Be sure to get the ball away quickly.

The best way to practice is to play catch with a receiver. Throw the ball, throw the ball, and throw it some more.

Daily Exercises

Push-ups develop arm and shoulder muscles. They will help to make you a better passer.

Lie facedown and place your hands beside your shoulders, palms down. Raise your body so you're resting only on your palms and toes. Hold it for a count of five. Lower your body and repeat the exercise.

To strengthen your wrists, do push-ups on your fists.

Don't neglect your stomach muscles. With a strong stomach you're less likely to feel it when you get tackled.

Leg lifts help build strong stomach muscles. Lie on your back, your heels touching the ground. Put your arms at your sides. Raise your feet about six inches. Then spread your feet apart. Hold this position for a count of five, then bring your feet together again. Lower your feet and then repeat the exercise.

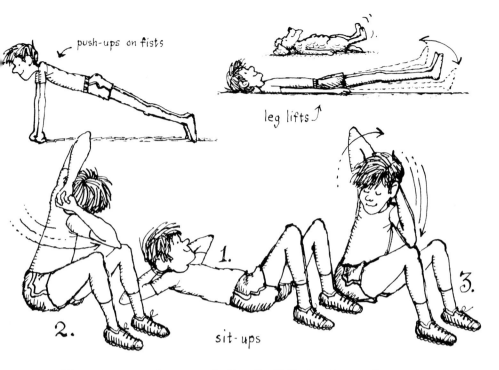

push-ups on fists

leg lifts ↗

1.

2.

3.

sit-ups

Sit-ups are also good for building stomach muscles. Lie on your back with your knees bent. Lock your fingers behind your head. Sit up; as you do, touch your right elbow to your left knee. Do it again, but this time touch your left elbow to your right knee. Keep repeating the drill. Try to do at least ten sit-ups.

Keeping Fit

You should also be working to improve your overall fitness. Do some running everyday.

After warming up, jog a lap around the school

track. Then walk a lap. Then alternately jog and walk several more laps. As you jog, keep aware of your running form. Be careful not to sway from side to side. Pump your knees high. Swing your arms back and forth. Keep your upper body erect.

Training With Weights

Weight training can also be helpful to you.

Weight training is different from weight lifting. In weight lifting, you try to lift the heaviest weight possible. In weight training, you use disk weights called barbells to strengthen certain muscles.

The amount of weight you lift isn't important. The exercise you do and the number of times you do it are what count. For example, to develop your wrists and forearms, do an exercise called the wrist curl. While standing, hold the barbell at thigh level, then simply raise it to shoulder level. You do not move your shoulders or upper arms. You do the exercise over and over again.

For more information about weight training, talk to your coach or gym teacher.

Footwork

The faster your feet are, the faster the rest of your body moves.

You have to be especially fast in darting back and setting up to throw. Several times a week, sprint backward as fast as you can. Do it several times. You don't have to sprint far, only ten or fifteen yards. Test yourself once a week to see whether your speed is improving.

Skipping rope is another good exercise for developing quick feet. It also helps to strengthen your wrists and hands. It improves your coordination. See how many times you can jump without missing. Try for fifty jumps, then try for one hundred.

Your Vision

You must be able to see teammates and opposing players to your right or left—without looking directly at them.

You can improve your range of vision with this drill: While looking straight ahead, put your right hand behind your right ear. Slowly bring the hand forward until you see it moving. But don't shift your eyes or turn your head. Try the same drill with your left hand. Do these exercises every day.

47

Your Voice

When calling plays, you need a strong voice, a loud voice.

If you're a person who speaks in a soft voice, try this exercise: Go someplace where you will be by yourself. Practice calling plays and signals at the top of your lungs.

Strategy

To choose the right play, you have to know the strengths and weaknesses of your team. For instance, one of your runners may not be fast, but offers good power. Another runner may be a speedster in the open field, but is easy to bring down. You have to weigh these factors in calling running plays.

As for your pass receivers, you should know the speed of each. You should know which ones are the best at cutting and faking. Some receivers are more sure-handed when running from right to left. Others prefer to go from left to right. You should be aware of such factors.

You must also study the opposition. Where are the weak spots in the line? Which defensive backs lack speed? Talk to your teammates. Learn all you can from them about the opposing players. Of course, your coach will also be giving you such information.

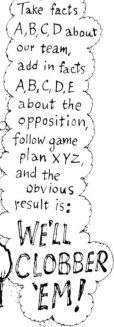

Take facts A,B,C,D about our team, add in facts A,B,C,D,E about the opposition, follow game plan XYZ, and the obvious result is: WE'LL CLOBBER 'EM!

STRATEGIST AT WORK

5 A Final Word

When his team wins, the quarterback gets cheered. When things go wrong, he hears boos. This happens, but it isn't exactly fair.

A quarterback can do only so much. His success depends on his teammates.

The quarterback is like the driver of a racing car. Without a good driver, the car won't go anywhere.

But the driver can't go anywhere without the car either. The best driver in the world can be knocked out of a race by a punctured tire or a breakdown. Just as the driver needs a sound car, so the quarterback needs a solid team. Sure, the quarterback is important, very important. But remember, football is never a one-man show.

About the Author

GEORGE SULLIVAN is a freelance writer with a number of sports books to his credit. In recent years, he has become interested in photography, and frequently takes the photographs he uses to illustrate his books. Mr. Sullivan was born in Lowell, Massachusetts, and received a Bachelor of Science degree from Fordham University. He lives in New York City with his wife and son.

About the Illustrator

DON MADDEN has both attended and taught at the Philadelphia Museum College of Art and has illustrated scores of children's books. Mr. Madden's work has received gold and silver medals at the Philadelphia Art Directors' Club exhibitions, and his work has been selected for reproduction in the *New York Art Directors' Annual,* in the international advertising art publication *Graphis,* and the *Society of Illustrators Annual.*

Mr. Madden lives with his wife, who is also an artist, and two children in upstate New York.